VERTIGO & GHOST

Bright Travellers

VERTIGO & GHOST

Fiona Benson

CAPE POETRY

1 3 5 7 9 10 8 6 4 2

Jonathan Cape, an imprint of Vintage,
20 Vauxhall Bridge Road,
London SW1V 2SA

Jonathan Cape is part of the Penguin Random House group of companies
whose addresses can be found at global.penguinrandomhouse.com

Penguin
Random House
UK

First published by Jonathan Cape in 2019

penguin.co.uk/vintage

A CIP catalogue record for this book is available
from the British Library

ISBN 9781787330818

Typeset in 11/13 pt Bembo by Jouve (UK), Milton Keynes
Printed and bound in Great Britain by TJ International Ltd, Padstow, Cornwall

Penguin Random House is committed to a sustainable future for
our business, our readers and our planet. This book is made
from Forest Stewardship Council® certified paper.

For Robin Robertson;
thank you for your courage,
and for helping me keep mine.

CONTENTS

PART TWO

PART ONE

ACE OF BASS

That was the summer
hormones poured into me
like an incredible chemical cocktail
into a tall iced glass, my teenage heart
a glossy, maraschino cherry
bobbing on top as that rainbow
shimmered through me, lighting me up
like a fish, and I was drunk,
obsessed, desperate to be touched,
colour streaming from my iridescent body

as the wide summer night threw open its doors
and called us into the evening to sit in its loveseat
and gossip about boys, though we'd have fucked
anyone back then – each other, had we dared,
right there on the tennis courts – all us unparented girls
released from the boarding house to *practise our backhand*,
desire between us like a shared addiction
in its crooked spoon, desire and the holding back,
the terrible restraint

as we listened to the top 40, or our three CDs
till the batteries ran down, till the asphalt's grit
had pressed its intricate red pattern on our thighs,
and we talked about who'd done what with whom
and how it felt, all of us quickening,
and sex wasn't here yet, but it was coming,
and we were running towards it,
its gorgeous euphoric mist;
pushing into our own starved bodies at night
for relief, like the after-calm might last,
like there was a deep well of love on the other side.

ZEUS

[Zeus]

days I talked with Zeus
I ate only ice
felt the blood trouble and burn
under my skin

found blisters
on the soft parts
of my body

bullet-proof glass
and a speaker-phone between us
and still I wasn't safe

thunder moved in my brain
tissue-crease
haemorrhage

I kept the dictaphone running
it recorded nothing
but my own voice
vulcanised and screaming
you won't get away with this

★

[archives]

Zeus on parole:

NO FUN
THIS ANKLEBAND
TAZERS ME
EVERY TIME
I BRUSH THE BOUNDS
AND YET IT IS
SHALL WE SAY
EROTIC?
ITS SUDDEN CURSE
ITS THRILL

★

[archives]

Zeus given
light sentence,
temporary gaol.
The judge delivers
that he is an exemplary member
of the swimming squad;
look at his muscular shoulders,
the way he forges through water;
as for the girl

★

[personal]

Rape is rarely
what you think.
Sometimes you are
outside yourself
looking down
thinking *slut*
as you let him do
what he wants
on your own familiar sheets
to stop the yelling
and the backhand to the face
and the zeroing in
of the fist.

★

[surveillance: track and field]

Zeus with his hair
in a golden tail
down at the running track
coaching girls.
Spikes on asphalt.
I WILL MAKE YOU AS FAST
AS SHOCK LIGHTNING
MY BEAUTIES
IF YOU LISTEN
IF YOU GROOM WELL

★

[surveillance: bull kneeling]

not there   dusk like a bruise   its yellow air
not there yet   some difficulty   in transmission
the near trees thrashing   and that thickening,
how it stirs   at the edge of the field   milk cows backed
against the furthest stile   stamping their hooves
like epileptics   drumming their heels   on the floor
nostrils frothing   the scorched white smell   of myrrh –
not there still   charcoal blur   manifesting
like a storm out at sea   bull on its knees   was it
was it flies?   staggers up   white bull smirched
lightning in his horns   phallus scarlet   and engorged
thunder crackles   on his suede   as he bellows
and the ground gapes   to the underworld   and all the dead
scream out   girl walking   by the river
drops her flowers and her phone   turns   starts to run

★

[Zeus]

I LIKE THESE MAGAZINES
YOU BUY HERA
YES   I LIKE THEM

LOOK AT THIS ONE
HER BIRD-FINE COLLARBONE
HER NIPPED-IN WAIST
LITTLE BABY-FACE

YOU'RE LOOKING HEAVY
IN THE STOMACH LATELY
YOU COULD DO SOME EXERCISE
ALWAYS LOUNGING AROUND
WITH THESE ZINES
LOOK AT YOUR WINGS

THOUGH YOU NEVER WERE
A PRETTY GIRL I SUPPOSE
THAT WAS NEVER
YOUR THING

★

[personal: speedo]

Before the beach
we stop
for a drink.
Zeus strips off
to a minuscule
red speedo
and bulges profanely.
I lapse my guard
and laugh
as he reclines
in the splay-legged
plastic chair.
It's a mistake.
He bolts upright.
I stir the ice
in my drink
and hold my breath
and listen
for the electricity
crackling across his skin
to rest.
Then I thank him
for the orange juice.
It's freshly pressed, I say,
the best I've ever tasted.
Zeus leans back once more
in his perilous chair
and watches
as the lovely nymphs
walk by
in neon bikinis,

the blades of their backs
shifting as they gesture
to each other.
I long to escape
in that conspiracy
of women.

★

[Zeus: anatomical dolls]

It's hard to explain. Let me show you
with the anatomical dolls. They have buttons for eyes
and details under their pants you wouldn't believe –
look underneath at the girl's folded labia, vagina,
the tucked-in silk-and-string umbilical
of a pull-down, poppet foetus, or the male's
miniature penis, his cotton-bag scrotum,
his sphincter ringed in little puckered stitches.
So the girl doll took off her frilly knickers
and the boy doll pushed down his trousers
and did this, and you might think it was love
if you hadn't seen Act One, the male doll
playing Punch, Judy trembling and bruised,
her bloody nose. Tell me what's the word for this,
this spreading of the legs and lips to delay violence,
and where's the rough music, all my charivari pots
and wooden spoons to out you Zeus,
to drive you through the streets, with songs
that find a name for you at last,
you filthy pimp, you animal, you rapist.

★

[personal]

He tracked me down
to Marylebone
with expensive flowers,
shouldered my bag
took my bike
and wheeled it,
while everyone around
smiled at his courtly manners.
No police on the concourse.
His grip on my arm
herding me home
to our single room.
I broke free and ran
with my ticket
through the barriers
onto the train.
How light I was.
How doubtfully safe.

★

[transformation: Nemesis]

I fled upriver
    cut gills, sprang scales,
        he was teeth in the water
          rudder-tailed –

I became a snake
    and hid on my belly
        he became a mongoose
          Rikki-Tikki-Tavi –

I became long-eared
    and burrowed into earth
        he was muscle in the tunnels,
          trap-jawed, fast –

I was a deer
    streaking for the hills
        he was the runner
          snapping at my heels –

I fletched black and tan
    and flew against the wind
        before I reached the stars
        he was swan, I was pinned –

we made a crater where we fell
    screaming through the night
        a bloody prolapse –
          his shame, not mine.

★

[Zeus: Danaë]

I LOVE THIS PRESIDENT.
HIS SHINY GOLD TOWER.
REMEMBER DANAË
I CAME TO HER
AS A SHOWER OF GOLD
WE TALK OF IT
AS CURRENCY
I WAS A CURRENT
RUNNING UP HER
A HARD AND MINTED
THING. HERE'S
HIS TOWER'S
GOLDEN PHALLUS
SUCH CHUTZPAH
I SHOULD SMITE HIM
BUT IT'S FUN
TO WATCH HIS WIFE
HER SMILE FALLING
AS HE LOOKS AWAY
IT'S A MEME
ON THE INTERNET
THE HUMANS
ARE ALSO AMUSED
BY THE SUGGESTION
OF ABUSE
A RICH WIFE'S CRIES
ARE A PARTICULAR SORT
OF INCENSE

COCAINE, PATCHOULI
THE WORLD
IS VIOLENT AND
RIDICULOUS AND SWEET

★

[Zeus: Semele]

DID I MENTION
SEMELE? DIED
IN FLAMES,
COULDN'T BEAR MY
TRUE IMMORTAL FORM
BEST TO DRESS
AS A PEACOCK A
BULL A STAG A SWAN
WHEN YOU WALK
AMONGST HUMANS
ESPECIALLY IF
YOU WANT
TO GET A GIRL

★

[transformation: Io]

CJD   Hera's gift
to   the luminous one
Io   groping down
the corridors   of the sanatorium

head swinging   like a lantern
unsteady legs   like a sick calf in mud
unable to piece   together   words
mah   she says   *mah*

at feeding time   she turns
from the spoon   tonguing it
bluntly   out   of her mouth
self-starved   here it comes

her pupils dilate   her brain
staggers   and deviates
down telescoping halls   protein folds
spongiform   she is goaded

she is goaded   and stung
god manifests   in thickening air
like a plague   like a locust swarm
he has   his dick   out

he will tear her   with his slimy mouth
he will   rip her apart
he is harm   she is smashing her head
against the wall   she is screeching

16 ·

at demons   doctors come running
she's buckled down   drugged calm
her father   weeps
is a river   of grief

her mother   stands behind
the reinforced glass   and will not turn
from her daughter's   slackening face
as it mouths   some blurred message

of violation   some plea   to come home
do not look   for beauty
it is gone   yet here's her father
stroking her hair   her mother

looking for   a cure   witnessing
insisting on   the gentlest care
see   how tenacious   they are
how truly   humans   love

★

[archives]

The day Zeus came to the safe-house
and shoved a sawn-off shotgun
through the letterbox   calling softly
like he was calling to the cat
that terrible croon,
SWEETHEART,
I'M HOME.

Had them kettled for hours.
Oh yes they were mightily changed.
Maddened, fuguing. Dissolved to rivers,
shaking like trees in a hurricane.
Some of them damaged in their entrails,
two thrown from high windows;
impossible to save.

★

[Zeus]

WHAT I LOVE:

THE MOMENT BEFORE DEATH
THAT CANDLE-SNUFF LOOK
AS THE FLAME BLACKS OUT
UNDER THE HOOD

ALL THE BRAIN CELLS
FLICKING OFF
LIKE SOMEONE THROWING THE LIGHTS
IN ONE LONG WAREHOUSE

FLICK   FLICK   FLICK   FLICK   FLICK

AND SEGMENT AFTER SEGMENT
OF THE WAREHOUSE DISAPPEARS
TILL THERE'S JUST THE BAND OF LIGHT
YOU STAND IN – BOOM!

I LIKE THAT MOMENT
OF EXTINGUISHMENT,
ITS HUMAN GONE.
I PEER INTO ITS DEEP WELL,

ITS TINY TRAIL OF STARS.
THIS IS THE LIQUOR
GODS LIVE FOR,
THIS TWENTY-ONE GRAMMES.

★

[Zeus addendum]

FORGOT TO SAY:
I LIKE THE INVOLUNTARY NOISES
HUMANS MAKE – CHILDREN –
THEIR HIGH-PITCHED SQUEAL
THAT GOES ON AND ON
BROKEN-NECKED RABBIT
IN THE FOX'S JAW
OR THE OLD ONES
THEIR GRAVELLY,
PURPLE-MORPHINE SNORE.

AND IF I WERE TALKING ABOUT BIRDS
I'D USE A DIFFERENT METAPHOR –
GRADATIONS OF DUSK,
ITS VIOLET GRAINS
DIMINISHING TO NOTHING
LITTLE BIRD CUPPED
IN THE HOLLOW OF MY PALM
ITS TINY QUENCH –
PHUT!
UNDER THE HOOD.

★

[forensics]

Zeus's cells
under the lens
comet-tailed
and coursing gold.
Corrosive.
Legion.

She staggers back
from the microscope
her lab-coat flapping
like a wounded swan
clutching her eye,
burned and acid-blind;

its retina
stark in her face,
a moon
she will not patch,
its wrinkled sclera
like egg skin,

or milky cellophane,
its inward watch —
the way she sometimes
sees the woman
before she bends
to the evidence,

down to what
she was wearing,
or the soil,

or the riverbed,
down to the very last things
she needed to tell.

She leaves it open wide,
her white eye
its lunar sheen.
Thinks: *Hera-screen*.

★

[Zeus: or, the problem with God]

I LIKE TO WATCH THE DOCTORS
IN THE EMERGENCY ROOM
WITH THEIR PADDLES –

SOME GONE SOUL
ALREADY CROSSED
BEYOND PRAYER

BUT HERE THEY ARE STILL AT WORK
AT THE HEART'S HEAVY MEAT
TRYING TO FORCE

THE DEAD ENGINE
TO TURN OVER
WITH A HORSE-KICK OF POWER

IT GIVES ME A FRISSON
TO SEE THE CORPSE
JOLT ON THE BED

I'VE ALWAYS APPROVED
OF THE ELECTRIC AGE
I COULD INSERT MY LIGHTNING BOLT

OF COURSE BUT I DON'T
ALL THOSE TUBES
AND THEIR GORGEOUS GOD MACHINE

COMING UP SHORT
UNFLATTERING
THAT ORACLE

THE FLAT-LINE

★

[transformation: Cyane]

Cyane – blue bruise of the aftermath, blue bruise of harm. The woman through whom the king of the underworld escaped: do not take that child from its mother – and he just blew through her like dynamite through water, the child raped in the locked adjoining room – Persephone in hell, or the war-stolen girl. *Let my teeth become water let my skin become water let my flesh become water let my bones become water* – Cyane, or a woman who's heard more than she can stand and takes herself to the well and drops herself in like a stone; heavy bullet, exit wound; Cyane: soiled water; the body in the well.

★

[not–Zeus: Medusa 1]

Poseidon the sea god
raped Medusa
where she prayed
in the temple of Athena

and Athena
cursed the girl
with a head full
of snakes.

I came to understand
rape is cultural,
pervasive;
that in this world

the woman is blamed.

★

[not–Zeus: Medusa 2]

Shunned girls sent
to the Magdalene laundries
their milk coming in,
newly stitched.

They will wash soiled sheets
till their chapped hands bleed in the lye;
till their backs are deformed;
till their hair turns white.

The priest will tell them
they're the devil's own whores,
that he's all around them,
hissing in their ears.

Meanwhile the nuns
will take their soft little babes
and bury them – the soft of them,
the down of them – in unmarked graves.

★

[not-Zeus: Medusa 3]

Daughter bound
and doused
in petrol

her brothers
red-eyed
and crazed

her father
jumping back
from the flames

as he drops
the lit match.
Her screaming flesh.

Her hair's bright snakes.
No balm for her,
your cinder daughter;

no water
for the hot coals
of her body.

My darling one
who laughed
like a woodpecker,

who loved
to lick the bowl
when I baked,

who stroked my back
when I cried,
my soft little child.

What mother
could walk
into that inferno now.

Still I try.

★

[closed circuit]

Zeus in the electric chair.
Madcapped, zapped,
at home in the lightning
no way to kill him,
monstrous, jiggered, laughing.

★

[surveillance]

Zeus under sedation.
IF YOU WOULD JUST MOVE
THAT FIRE HYDRANT
I COULD SEE
THE VIRGINS BATHING.
OH HERA.

★

[transformation: Daphne]

Who roots, flares into leaf, becomes tree.
But in the change before the change
Zeus's son courses her like a hound
and Daphne is a hare, trying to leap free.
That day at the races a whippet lost its head
in the hold, its cries leaking out of the dark trap
like poisoned milk. Then *clank* and all the gates
lifted, and the dogs streaked out, hurtling after
a dummy on castors, which rattled over the sleepers
of a long, greased rail. The pack was an unreadable blur.
Once it was over, handlers hooked their legs
over the barrier and came for their dogs,
clipping on each leash. Zeus behind the scenes:
his electric-shock collar, his snippets of meat.
Out beyond the pale there's no straight course,
just waterlogged fields and Daphne's hectic
blurts of speed. She's at the edge of her wits,
retching with fear, and he is *everywhere*,
stumbling her up, ahead of her, above,
his stink, his spit; he hollers and barks
in the rough of his throat, cuffs out her legs
from under her, tears at her flanks with his teeth
but still delays, and still she doubles back
and jinks and feints and flees.
By nightfall she is ragged in her hind-end,
blood-ebbed and frayed and wanting to be gone
into the gentleness, though there's this bright light,
this dazzle in her eyes, that won't let her sleep.
She cries for her daddy like any other girl
who's run beyond her strength, whose heart has failed.

When a hare dies it screams like a mortal child.
Disconcerted, Apollo looks up from the field.
There's Zeus in the dark holding the lamp,
keeping it steady for the rape, and the kill.

★

[screenplay]

Zeus rattling his tin cup
on the bars of his cell
    CUT TO:
Zeus in the exercise yard
looking up through rain
his upturned face, his smile
    CUT
(Zeus who can walk between raindrops
without getting wet
who can pass through the vaults
and walls of this prison
as if they were air
who could pour himself
between the atoms.
You've got to ask
why he's here?)
HERA.

★

[Zeus: oubliette]

Oubliette –
dry, rough-sided well
you're shoved down
landing in the broken crockery
of your own bones
your inward mulch.
Nothing to drink
though your voice
plays the shaft
so tenderly
calling for
a wet rag to suck
a crumb, a rope;
no rat daughter
to morsel you home,
huis clos.
Understand: you
are the oubliette's
best catch
being immortal, undying;
trapped like a crayfish
in its crate
socked at the bottom
of a starless lake,
or this long hole
in the under-web
where we shove
our worst psychoses,
our soiled, repugnant
images.
Blood pools

                    under your skin,
                    indelible ink,
                    tablecloth stain;
                    the point of this
                    not, after all,
                    occlusion,
                    but suffering.

                              ★

[surveillance]

Zeus hooked up to an oxygen tank
covering the tracheotomy in his throat to talk
his voice somewhere between
motor-rev and burp;
who has a scarf round his neck
so you don't see the hole;
who still asks,
WOULDN'T YOU LIKE
TO GO FOR A WALK?
THERE'S SOMEWHERE PRIVATE
I KNOW PRETTY GIRL

                              ★

[transformation: Callisto]

Split urethra, fistula, stitched rectum.
Infant removed *for its own protection.*
Her breasts are searing bags of milk,
her shirt is soaked. She will not talk.
Her mother takes her home, coaxes her to eat,
roasts chicken with potatoes, herbs and salts the skins.
Callisto picks the carcass clean, moves on –
pork chops, dumplings, chouquettes, quenelles,
past repletion, through to the distended gullet,
forced stomach, goose with a funnel down its throat
and the grain shovelled in with a scoop,
beak tied shut, liver warped.
She holds herself down, clamps her mouth,
piles on flesh like upholstery,
does violence to herself, cuts, infected sores,
squats to shit does not wipe does not wash
her hair down her back in a matted clump,
her hunch and look-away demeanour delivering her over
onto all fours, patchy fur, hardened claws.
Her mother searches in the dark –
every doorway and underpass.
Finds her daughter mite-ridden and stubborn.
Callisto I love you come home.
Cornered by a ranger one morning Callisto
rakes at the air with her paws, is chased out of town
with tranq guns and flares, their falling coals like meteors.
But there is pleasure in the woods –
the sun shining amber on her fur,
the teeming world of the river as she hunts headlong
after fish, or shins up a tree tracking bees
and bites through the sugared wax crust

to the golden ooze of the honey. She grooms herself
with a rasped tongue, heaving her body over
to reach her belly. There are moments in her cave
when she almost feels safe, and sleeps to dream
of the cub who mewed at her briefly before he was taken;
his eyes swollen shut from the pressure of birth,
his small blind face searching for her voice,
his kicking legs and his tiny fists waving.
Bundled out of the room. Perfect human.
Her voice, when she calls for him,
is the voice of her own mother, weeping.
Go ahead, Zeus. Constellate this.

★

[surveillance]

Zeus watching carp in the hospital pond
on Zenuphlate, Zemperon X, Zanutax.
Getting an erection through the haze
shifting back and forth,
fidgeting with his slacks,
distressed.
The psych nurse brings pills
in a doll-sized paper cup.
These are for you Zeus.
Hold out your tongue.
What nymphs go dancing in your brain,
what tortures?
I WILL RAPE A CHILD WITH AN IMPLEMENT
AND THAT IMPLEMENT WILL BE SWAN.

★

[surveillance]

Thunder, immanence.
I hunch under the faint
drip drip of rain,

escort my toddler
who is puddle-stomping
and oblivious.

I have lost us
our immunity
and I am afraid.

Who will know
if lightning strikes
that punishment was due?

All round me
in the heavy air
watching, Zeus.

★

[Daughter of Zeus: Pallas Athena]

Someone else's Zeus
shit-faced at the school gates,
crouched to level
with his daughter's pallid face,

whispering, wheedling,
a shout he reins back in . . .
She's dancing
on the tight leash of his attention,

like a little yellow vixen
caught by her throat in a snare,
writhing like a flame
of pale yellow fire –

she'll break her mouth
trying to chew through
that ferrous loop
of love and sorrow –

from those sown teeth,
their perimeter of tears,
a warrior a warrior
a warrior will rise.

★

[votive]

Hera vouchsafe.
Vouchsafe our children in the world.
Keep him in the prison of your vigilance.
Make sure. Hold.

★

[translation from the annals: Ganymede]

I was sent for the interrogation. Ganymede's mother
was old now and dying, still trundling the moors
looking for remains. He was her darling boy,
her joyful one, and she appealed often on television.
Everyone who saw her wept.
I had not been in proximity with the Powers before,
and was afraid of their full-skin tattoos and body-jewels
and their ease with weapons. I did not fully understand
their dialect, and between themselves they talked
in an ancient language of the seraphim.
The scars down their backs were infected
and larval, pursed at the seams and radiating heat;
when we left earth's atmosphere, blades flicked out
like wings. The flight took months,
and the rations set aside for my use were poor.
I became weak and slept a great deal
and had bad dreams. Sometimes I'd wake
soaked in sweat and hear the Powers singing
on a scale other than our own, high and screeching,
vibrating in a way that made me heave up yellow bile.
At the seventeenth swing of the magnetic field
we came to the forest. It wasn't as I'd imagined.
Chains ran through the vacuum, taut as plumb-lines,
though I couldn't tell how they were pinned,
and the cables screamed as solar winds
tore round the vast, uneasy fleet.
Each cell was stalled mid-air like an elevator.
I caught glimpses of the prisoners – bare teeth at the bars,
each cage a bloodied hutch; a few on the outskirts
seen close-up – Ixion starved, high-stepping,
lifting his shanks on the spot

treading an invisible wheel; a daughter drowning
in a Perspex tank, her feet tipping the bottom
like a dancer on pointe endlessly missing her step –
we would not treat an animal this way.
I felt the Powers watching me, my own sins appraised.
Zeus had been dismembered and set in separate cages
out beyond the perimeter – an Egyptian trick.
We hauled them up two at a time checking the inventory
then lifted the parts I needed last, the voice-box
and mouth with its palate intact, its teeth and lips
and clamped tongue, then the pink-grey brain,
the dark heart creeping across the floor of its cage
with each systolic thump, smearing blood like a badly
    beaten rat.
The tongue was released from its bit, and was swollen
but intelligible to the Powers who said it was talking
in curses and spells. The pieces would not yield
the boy's location, though the synapses of the brain
lit up like a firework display when questioned.
The parts whistled to one another
like abusive masters to their kicked-in, wary dogs,
some 'come-to-heel', some barely stifled threat
and the cages themselves began to agitate and sing
and I became something beyond afraid.
The Powers sent the pieces hurtling back,
set at massive intervals, galaxies estranged.
They were swallowed into the leagues as if by ink.
And still the cables rattled and shook, and still I am afraid.

★

PART TWO

DEAR COMRADE OF THE
BOARDING HOUSE

This is the poem in which your jeep does not crash;
the roads are not potholed dirt, a goat does not
wander into your path, your husband does not
startle and swerve but ploughs on and kills the goat
with its ticks and famished udders, or better yet,
the goat skitters back into the brush; at any rate,
your jeep does not turn or if it turns
it is so well equipped with airbags and seatbelts
that you are not harmed, or if you are harmed
this poem is the hospital in which you are healed
it is so well stocked with blood and drugs and sterilised needles,
not the outback village hospital with its supplies depleted
and its long row of malarial sleepers, its single frightened doctor
looking grave; and you do not know you are dying,
so do not tell your husband that you hope your death at twenty-five
will bring your friends to God, an evangelist to the end;
well here I am, praying as best I can for a poem in which
you do not crawl back to me night after night for fifteen years
returned but changed, disfigured or shaven-haired,
held hostage or raped, a little simple now,
unable to tell me about the atrocities you've suffered
on the other side; and I hold your damaged body
in my arms for a single, split second, before I wake
to this unresurrected world in which you are still
practically a schoolgirl, dear comrade,
and never anything but dead.

TWO SPARROWS

i

My heart is for the sparrow, taken outside
my kitchen window in its chocolate hood,
already elect, condemned, as it picks about
on the patio's top step, grabbed at the neck
by the hawk, which turns and is gone
before the sparrow-flock even begins to rupture,
scattering in slow-time, only now seeing
that the raptor has been amongst them.
Years back I saw a sparrow play with a feather
on the old flat roof of our house – catch and release
with its beak, over and over, a spirit at play.
God says even these small ones are numbered,
but the flock, now hopping about like fleas,
can't seem to figure which one of them's gone,
and the nameless dead of the human world
float endlessly down the corpse-choked river,
and I'm not sure of anything anymore,
least of all benevolence, or God.

ii

A repeated thud – that sparrow somehow lost
to its flock, tilting itself at the kitchen window,
launching its beak like a needle, as if it meant
to pierce the pane, where it sees, reflected, the hedge
held in such a liquid depth – redoubled,
intense, a shimmering, demoiselle green.
I try to shoo it off, and the bird pauses stunned
with its wings fanned out on the hot ground
and its beak forked, panting, its dry tongue flickering
before it starts again, expecting each time
a give in the pane, as if that hard, concussive glass
might suddenly part and let him in
to his heart's own kingdom, the true empyrean,
where a long-lost fellowship of souls
throngs in the lush slaked leaf to welcome him.

Beauty fails. Here's the aftermath –
Autumn's slump, all the berries summer
left on the thorn shrivelled, and grown
a fur pelisse like tiny mice;
under the hedge, that smell of shit.
You chose this. Each walk is damp and slick.
And yes, there will be frost, its crisp white hoar's
bright diamond; but first, mucky skies
the sulks, the year's downturn as winter shuts
like a trap, its narrow light, and you are caught
by sadness. What would you do, would you fly
with the swallows, summer's Bedouins,
moving their tents between the constellations?
Get on your knees. Remember that you chose.

★

Search in the dirt for one small thing:
A scabbed and jewelled mould, or yellow snail,
its horns tender as mushroom caps,
its shell tilting gold like a buttercup
as it oozes along a rotting stalk –
even its slime is luminous.
Redeem the day, because you chose this,
the forest and the solitude, the river
with its doped-up banks of balsam
and the constant squabble of the goldfinch charm
feasting in the thistles, the docks, the nettles,
you chose all this, you chose to immerse yourself
in green, to go where people rarely come,
its yours, you rich and shivering hedge-tramp, Queen.

ALMOND BLOSSOM

This morning, love, I'm tired and grave;
I can barely hear the wintered bird's small song
over the hum of the central heating.
We must trust, I suppose, to the song's bare minim:

that spring will be a green havoc
as the trees burst their slums
and the dirt breaks open to admit
crocus-spear and cyclamen;

and though we can't yet feel it
earth's already begun
her slow incline, inch by ruined inch,
easing you back from the brink.

FLY

Spring broke out but my soul did not.
It kept to sleet and inwards fog.
Forget-me-nots around the path,
a speckled thrush; I spoke rarely
and had a sour mouth. I couldn't make love.
My husband lay beside me in the dark.
I listened till he slept. I picked out
all the bad parts of my day like sore jewels
and polished them till they hurt.
I wanted to take myself off like a misshapen jumper,
a badly fitting frock. I wanted
to peel it off and burn it in the garden
with the rubbish, pushing it deep
into the fire with a fork. And what sliver
of my stripped and pelted soul there still remained,
I'd have it gone, smoked out, shunned,
fled not into the Milky Way,
that shining path of souls, but the in-between,
the nothing. But this overshoots the mark,
this gnashing sorrow, so Wagnerian;
it was more a vague, grey element I moved in
that kept me remote and slow,
like a bound and stifled fly, half-paralysed,
drugged dumb, its soft and intermittent buzz,
its torpid struggle in the spider's sick cocoon.
What now if I call on the sublime?
What bright angels of the pharmakon
will come now if I call, and rip
this sticky gauze and tear me out?

TOAD

Toad fat toad,
fleshed round
diminutive bones,

forearms and thighs
even at rest
corded, grotesque,

beaded, bitter skin
the crows must strip
like toxic braille,

downturned mouth and jowl,
the round eye's horizontal slit,
its shimmering gold foil.

Toad with all her trappings.
Wedged under a slate lip
of the garden wall.

Dead but for
the bubble at her throat,
inflating now and then

like clear stretched gum,
its giveaway, insistent pulse.
Toad, my best familiar.

Hard to believe in stirring, sister,
hard to believe
in the light at all

when each day is a cold stone
you must push,
and there is no jewel.

Still you persist.
Spring could be
a sunlit, green,

effervescent swim
through weed
and spawn.

Perhaps this is only
purgatory, sister,
and beyond it, bliss.

AFTER THE FLOOD

The ranch is a scorched morgue —
trees turned wrangler,
cattle caught
at the height of gone water —

heavy bull
pegged in the fork
of a slender eucalyptus
as if it soared —

strange place for a cow to roast
on its silly spit —
what terrifying butcher
hung you up

in this bad pantry
with its stinking song
of sour meat and jelly,
and your thick tongue hatching

in a petrol-blue revolution
as fly-storms
take their chainsaws
to your simmered corpse.

HARUSPEX

October and the blown
mushroom dissolves,
its volva clubbed,
its stalk and cap,
its singed and musky gills.

I've spent too long collapsed
over this inwards dark
disembowelled, gone
to ground, fingering
my own wet spills

and bodily secretions,
a dream in which
I am fucking and weeping –
my mind has been wrong
for a long long time.

Here is its fruit.
It is true,
I hear voices
and talk to myself.
I am done with shame.

BEATITUDE (*AH! BRIGHT WINGS!*)

Sad, agnostic soul, I go down to the river
and swim beyond the fence-line, trespassing,
water cold and sweet at the nape of my neck,
every nerve alert, and I watch the martins'
whiplash, loopback flight, their scourge
of insect cumuli, that harried, brittle meat.
The sandy bank is riddled with their nests,
each hole a snug of sun-warmed young,
and the long ledge thrums with storeyed wings.

The martins weigh anchor across the sky
as if they're trying to catch down heaven –
and now it seems that heaven is upon us
like some vast and open canvas, love flung down
in the willows' shivering intervals, their bright
and pliant stems falling like green rain;
and I'm carried by the river, numb with cold,
a compass to the currents, briefly healed.

WHITE NOSE DISEASE

The bats
are infected,
muzzled in fungus

their snouts
webbed over
with spores –

a surgical mask
grown over the face,
a groping, floury gauze.

They fall
in their wintering
millions,

but all encrypted
beyond our watch
so we come

in the spring
and find them gone,
their bones underfoot

in drifts,
the cave roof desolate
in our breath's white mist.

ECTOPIC / YELLOW SEAHORSE

Erupted through
the fallopian tube,
out-of-womb,

like a rare fish grown
in a city drainpipe,
a yellow seahorse

keeping hold
on the wind-sworn rooftops.
Far below

the sirens
and the lovely chains
of light.

The ornate
slipknot
of your tail

is clinched
on impacted litter
and your spine unfurls

like coral, or sea-thorn,
embedded, infected,
doubling me over,

yet who wouldn't want
the tiny, scripted architecture
of your trunk,

your fluted snout,
and your embryonic heart
galloping in the face

of the sky's dry machinery,
its mills and presses,
its whirling batteries.

It will beat you out,
turn you to salt
till you are

the world's rarest mineral,
its slightest revenant.
And here is that storm again,

wrenching at your roots,
insisting that you fly now
little horse, little flower,

into the dark,
its million
whistling stars.

BLUE HERON

A year of losing everything, hard,
      your father gone, a baby who won't be born.
            I think of you far off in the Canadian North
            running through the marsh,
      the reeds ramped in slicks and rotting,
the boardwalk slippy underfoot –

the blue heron doesn't move
      though you pass almost close enough to touch;
            he's bound in his blood
            to the slow, hunched river-work of grief,
      invisible, mantled in stillness
watching the shadow-play of fish.

Ice is really coming on now,
      stiffening the shallows to opaque schist,
            and above you in the freezing zones
            the last of the departed souls
      are hoarding for the end migration,
the world resolving under them

into fields of loss or magnetism.
      I pray you not to slip.
            I pray the blue heron to lift
            and span the tight pressed feathers of his wings
      lapis, cobalt, mazarine –
for should the blue heron lift

looking for a break in the bare-string willow –
        should the blue heron lift
                from the tightening shallows
                there will be love, release;
        look now at the white stars falling,
the night-sky-blue of heron, rising.

SONG FOR THE RABBIT MAN

The butcher's back, tying his knots
in the hedge. His red-eyed ferret
pours itself down rabbit-holes,
flushing out the burrows,

their many exits mined and countermined –
a warren's an exploded wound –
tick-tock, tick-tock, the ferret seeks,
all the slip-routes noosed, besieged,

the whole ridge seined
by the butcher's clever hands.
Through naked thorn I catch
the long, balletic arc

of an oatmeal-coloured buck
the butcher holds at his waist.
Back at his shop he eases each corpse
out of its coat like a lover,

tender to all the weeping cisterns of the body,
the slick little heart,
the bladder's pissy sac,
the sphincter's slender wedding band.

Dusk at the hedge and the doe
inches out of her nest.
Her horseshoe womb is a sharp new moon,
seven kits are ripening in seven rooms.

The buck's lean meat
with its dark placental taste of roots,
is iron on the tongue,
a quick thing gone, beginning.

WILDEBEEST

I became beest –
I submitted to my body's
wild stampede
to deliver you safe
to the other side

and I was both the flood
and the furious corral
from which you were expelled –
trampled and pressed
and hammered like metal,

almost crushed
in that torrent of muscle,
its coursing rift –
I couldn't not push –
stretching and scalding

as if I were giving birth
to some fierce, Taurean star
spoked at the rim,
thorned like the sun –
and I tore

as you crowned
with your fist
beside your face –
slick little wildebeest,
hoof-first, doused –

how I arched
trailing you behind me,
my half-born calf
unfolding
like sharp origami

then falling in a hot
and slippery rush
to be brought from water
now ruddled with blood
and laid on my breast –

dark-haired like your sister,
incarnate, loved.

AFTERBIRTH

Squatting, again –
this time over the toilet
to rinse –

sweet stink
of torn labia
under warm water

poured
from a re-used
plastic bottle,

its acid sting.
Ragged animal
I stagger back

to my bed –
smell of blood
all over the ward

its kingdom
of excrement
and offal

my stomach
a flaccid bag
beginning to shrivel

milk squeezed
from my breasts
in a sore yellow paste

all this for the stranger
sleeping
in the crib.

PLACENTA

This is yours
and none of mine –
your outer organ,
unwieldy carry-on,
bio-convertor, generator,
meaty battery-pack.

I'm drawn
to its ridged outer labyrinth,
my womb's bright negative,
its intimate, violet latch;
and the cord, which is sinewy,
and kinked, and fat.

Here's the answer
to all your body's failures –
the gluey tapioca
of grey cells
that grow to bone,
stem cells that mend organs

and tissue and nerve –
this is your heal-all,
your infinite cure.
We weigh it,
we take it to the furnace
to be burnt.

IN THE MILK DAYS OF YOUR SISTER

After years of ruling this roost, little chick,
your hair is un-brushed,
your breakfast brought in to the sitting room,
everything out of custom

and your parents somehow gone,
your father silent, the laughter
blown out of your mother
like someone snuffed her out.

You put your hands
each side of your sister's fat cheeks
in a gesture entirely your own,
and you tell her that you love her,

and my poor exhausted soul
for love of you, bows down.

DAUGHTER DROWNING

My daughter slipped on wet tiles into the pool,
calling through the water as she fell,
windmilling up with her chin thrown back
then going under, forgetting to tread water
or look about her, drowning within reach of the ledge.
I plunged through the shallows and caught her up;
she was spouting like a gargoyle,
spluttering and weeping, clinging to my neck.
Now she's trying to get me to look,
and I almost can't do it, some weird switch flipped
that means I watch the new-born like a hawk
afraid she'll forget to breathe, or her heart will stop
or she'll choke on her own tongue if I look away,
even for a second. Meanwhile here's the first-born
fighting for attention, as if it were oxygen
and she were drowning, as if she had dropped
through unfathomed water, and her mother
were a long way off, and hadn't even seen her
start to slip.

RUINS

Here's my body
in the bath, all the skin's
inflamed trenches
and lost dominions,

my belly's fallen keystone
its slackened tilt –
for all the Aztec gold
I'd not give up

this room where you slept,
your spine to my right,
your head
stoppered in my pelvis

like a good amen –
amen I say
to my own damn bulk,
my milk-stretched breasts –

amen I say to all of this
if I have you –
your screwball smile
at every dawn,

your half-pitched, milk-wild smile
at every waking call,
my loved-beyond-all-reason
darling, dark-eyed girl.

TERMITE QUEEN

Down in the boiler room
this ikon, this body-locked Queen,
trapped in her labours and suffering,
her milky birth canal
plunging and bucking,
oozing and erupting,
pulsing eggs,
whilst her little-girl head
and six legs dangle,
the way the hands
of the morbidly obese
hang so small and impotent,
her tiny, useless feet.

She's grown too large for the tunnels
and even should the red ants come
she could not leave this urgent dungeon.
Her mate strokes her back
and scurries across her glistening abdomen
to enter the glans again and again –
pheromone-head, all he wants to do
is heavy-pet or fuck.
Workers feed her at the mouth
and excavate the room
to accommodate her girth;
when she dies
they will lick her up.

Beyond her in the city
her eggs are hatching in the nurseries,
her workers are tending to gardens and barns,
and hundreds of floors up

the cooling-tower breathes
blue, unchambered air –
which the Queen flew through
in that first strange dream of thermals
she navigated lightly, easily,
back in the termite storm
when they all had wings,
when they all unlatched them prettily
and burrowed down.

MOON

Leave my backbone for the children –
like a cutting hung in a jar of mucky water
though I have never taken one – no –
not even a geranium, that simple clone
blooming year on, but the moon –

its walls hacked out by dark
to a thin rind still grows back,
luminous and full, a miracle,
as if a whole orange grew
from a slice of peel –

not the half-spun eggs in me
their quiet requests for clemency,
their human code expelled in blood –
I am near the end of child-bearing,
but in our fat gravidity we ate stars

like plump white grubs and licked our lips
and bloomed with life; the tap of a nail
against the taut skin of my belly
brought the answering sweep
of my daughter's knee

right here below my diaphragm;
what it was to be full,
to be huge in the sky
like the blessed moon,
its counter-pull, its light.

CELLS

These are the *chimera* –
foetal cells
that migrate across the placenta
and bed down
even in the mother's brain.

Straight-off I thought of that robot car
driven by a web of neurons
extracted from a rat
and grown on silicone,
electrode-primed.

The rat-brain drove the car
and the car spun its wheels
and went mad –
shunting into corners,
cowering under the scientist's chair –

behaving like a rat
that found itself exposed
and sought concealment.
It knew it was out in the open.
It did not know it was dead.

As for my daughters' cells
left stashed in my body
like stowaways or spies,
I think they pilot me
into agonies of protection –

'it's not my own mortality
I flail at now, but theirs.
Look how fitfully I steer,
how obsolete I am in person;
I am wheeled and governed.

LOVE POEM, LUCCA

All week I'm drawn to the watchtower.
It has trees springing out of its head
like a tall, brick vase of forest.
I want to go up. I insist.
We climb two hundred winding stairs
to the lovely, green, oak-tree crown
where, of course, I fail –
the four walls sledging off through space
have me utterly wasted, wanting
to spread headlong on my belly
and grip the bricks with my nails,
even then caught in the vertical fall
of the avalanche, its hollow core.
How could the trees root here?
We've brought up our girl.
She ricochets between the ledge
and the steep of the stair like a firework
in a confined space, half crazed,
about to fall. I cannot look.
Here is James scooping us up –
his trembling, ghost-faced wife,
his fearless, wayward daughter –
guiding us back down the steps.
So much for the tower
like a beautiful red elevator.
So much for the sunlit view
of the hills beyond, or the city walls,
all the red roofs crowded in-between
like boats in haven. I stay close
to my husband, I hold his hand.
Listen, child: he's the sure
and steady ground; because of him
we live.

PORTRAIT OF OUR DAUGHTERS

Like baby elephants, their ears and tails
are distinctive; witness their naked rumps
on the June lawn as they sport with water to cool down.
Their happiness too is elephantine – they sing
silly songs, snorkel and spout fountains,
then hurl themselves about on the trampoline
to get dry. We are nothing to them till they fight –
then there is barging and squeaking and they need us
to intervene. The cause, of course, is bewildering.
But finally they're assimilated back,
a herd unto themselves, kicking up the grass,
their strange, endangered joy trumpeted
for miles as they streak across the garden,
our crazy girls, our glorious, stampeding calves.

MENINGITIS

My grandmother, diminished in her bones,
loyal to her large-print Mills & Boon
and her soaps, bent perpendicular over her zimmer,
weeping, still weeping for her daughter June,
who was *sweet, so sweet*, the child of her heart –
soft blonde curls and forget-me-not eyes,
gentle and kind – how June took care of the evacuees,
holding out their towels as they stepped
from the disinfectant bath to be deloused.
How, after all that – the World's War
and its shell-shocked peace, the Mickey Mouse
gas mask packed away at last, June
went to bed with half a soluble aspirin
for a headache and by the morning was gone.
The way my grandmother tells it, she didn't know
there was anything out of the ordinary wrong,
and June died in the night in wet sheets, alone,
as the terrible roses bloomed beneath her skin.
My grandmother out of her mind with pain,
writhing and kicking on the kitchen linoleum,
while my uncle as a boy watched on.
Which is why my father came to be born,
to bring her back to the living, a baby to hold.
And this is my inheritance, this heirloom of grief:
the way my daughters' fevers crush me,
how I check their skin obsessively
for tell-tale burns, how I scoop them
out of the flames where the devil eats them,
daughter like a hot poultice I hold
against my frightened heart, the marks I make

above my door that the angel of the plague
might pass, where my grandmother waits,
standing on the threshold in her red velour slippers,
unable to step over, peering fearfully into the dark.

HEAVENLY BODIES

Small mother, I want to believe
that when the soul is released
it is borne to the stars by a swan,
though the body remains, your small bones laid
in a Perspex kist and soft-clothed clean,
beads at your mouth like a song for the child
curled at your side on a dead swan's wing.
Lately I learned that, for another tribe,
Ursa Major constellates a stretcher
and Ursa Minor is the stretcher of a child.
Surely your baby was flown on this soft litter
to the emergency room of heaven,
hurtled through its vast swing doors
into galleries of light, nursed
and cauterised, without trembling or pain.
Some hot Syrian nights
of bomb-shocked children shivering in the clinic,
legs dangling from the gurney, screaming
for a mother who is not there,
a small boy cradling his baby sister
who is dead, I want more than anything
to trust that a child's soul flies up
on a swan's white back, that there's room for them all
in the deep expanding dark, that they'll take
their stations, their heavenly bodies burning,
and graze the world again, as light.
But I think this life is all there is,
and all these children know of it
is a doctor whose hand shakes so much
she cannot stitch, and a cold faraway feeling,
the white rush of a white breath leaving
and the strange ascension of dying.

VILLAGE

I walked up and up. Thought the same cracked thoughts
about the same cracked stuff: ego, work –
why hadn't I been published in this, invited to that,
yak yak yak, meanwhile shrapnel, exile,
the bombed, the drowned; tent cities that stretch for miles.
I left the kids yelling blue murder,
left them to their father, slammed the door, walked fast.
My halfway mark is a wind-pruned beech,
and each dipped illuminated leaf was twisting
like holy fire in the last rays of the sun
as its wheel slipped low over the horizon.
I already toiled in the lane-trough's early dusk,
for all the lanes are high-hedged here and thoroughfare
to the immortal geometries of flies, scribbling
their pentagrams and signs invisibly on air.
That beech was the last lit tree in the universe,
and it sang with a strange and lonely friction to the sun,
some *don't be gone*, some treaty for the dawn.
I walked up to the galvanised steel gate
and hoiked myself over and found myself watched
by a large buck rabbit drumming his foot
on the hard red dirt, a colony alert.
Here was the rapeseed in fluorescent bloom,
leguminous and sprung, its acid yellow lime
erupting into beauty. Always the urge
to lie down here and tryst, away from crowded rooms
and all their petty navigations; to lie down
headlong with my lover, to open for the deepest kiss.
The rabbit turned its long white scut
into the rapeseeds' wiry wood and disappeared.
I trespassed the whole wild edge of the field
and found the farmer's timber stacked in long,

sawn cords, seasoning for next year's fires,
and in amongst it woodlice, their soft and huddled shells
a useless sort of shield, and milky spores of mould,
cantilevering the bark in secret, wood–dark coombs.
There's nowhere safe in the world for an exiled child.
I could see my village held in the crook of the valley
along the dwindled stream; the children
were simmering down, getting into bed;
the men were reading them stories, kissing their heads.
And I felt love for my small and human life down there,
its tenderness.

HIDE AND SEEK

After her swim I wrap my child warm
and take her to the changing room
and lay her down to dry. She holds the corners
of the towel up over her face
like a soft, turquoise tent and yells
'Hide and seek! Hide and seek!'
I lift an edge and shout 'Boo!'
and she shrieks with laughter –
I can feel the heat rising from her body
and smell the chlorine – she hides again,
and again I peek under and she's beside herself
with happiness – she's at an age where she thinks
that if she just stands still in the middle of the lawn
I will not see her, that somehow she is gone –
but always, in the pockets behind this game,
there is this residue, this constriction,
families squeezed behind false walls
or hidden under the floor. I think of the soldier
sensing the hollow under his sole
and prying up the board on all those cramped
and flinching humans; but mostly I think
of the mothers, their hearts jumping out of their mouths
trying to shush their children – my first-born now,
who's never been able to do as she's told,
how she'd have writhed and screamed and bitten like a cat
if I'd tried to hold her quiet, how I'd have hurt her,
clamping her mouth, trying to keep her still.
The trapdoor is always opening, the women and children
are herded into the yard – and I ask myself if,
when my daughters were pulled from me,
I would fight and scream to keep them,
or let them go gently, knowing

there was nothing to be done?
If we were pushed into the showers
would I pretend it was only time to get them clean?
We are not meant to write of the Sho'ah,
we who were not there, but on bad days it's all I can think of,
the mothers trying to shield their children with their bodies
under the showers, screaming for mercy, begging for rain.
And it's never over – here are the children
riding to the border in fridges as the air becomes hot and thin,
their tiny bodies glowing like bright sardines
on the custom officer's hand-held scan;
and here is the tribesman carrying your husband's genitals
and a bloody machete, and you are a mother
running for your life with a baby tied to your back
and two children by the hand
but one small son is falling behind;
Jesus fucking Christ, I don't know who
I'm teaching you to hide from, but look
how eagerly you learn.

WOOD SONG

Daughters, when they come
we will hide in the forest,
we'll cross the meadow
and the orchard,

their shifting rooms,
till we are deer in the woods —
the quick-footed hind
and her fawns —

and we'll slip through the thickets
or take the water's scentless course,
and follow the lichen
brightening north,

and I'll keep you warm
where we nest
beneath the bracken's
tangled roof,

and in the morning when we wake
we will move, move, move,
beneath the dark forgiving hand
of the clouds,

with the slightest weather
moving on,
and when our feet fall
they will fall like rain,

and there will be no catching us,
and no harm will come,
so keep close daughters
in the woods where we run,

for we are tracks in the dew
vanishing at dawn,
we are mist, we are rain,
we are gone.

MEXICAN FREE-TAIL BATS

Now it comes back,
the free-tail kits
falling through

the nacred dark
to the guano floor,
its acid phosphorescence.

They stagger on their wing-tips
like haunted little veterans
trying to crutch themselves

out of the sewage,
the dead-lands,
and the insects fetch them down.

The mother bat swoops in
from harvesting
amongst the stars

her belly full of moths,
her body spinning milk,
moon-pale, cream-rich.

She sweeps the cave roof
again and again
listening for her kit,

its particular pitch
until she is
a black glove of panic

dervishing under
the seething roost,
its million singing fruit:

not here; not here.

EUROFIGHTER TYPHOON

My daughters are playing outside with plastic hoops;
the elder is trying to hula, over and over –
it falls off her hips, but she keeps trying,
and the younger is watching and giggling,
and they're happy in the bright afternoon.
I'm indoors at the hob with the door open
so I can see them, because the elder might trip,
and the younger is still a baby and liable to eat dirt,
when out of clear skies a jet comes in low
over the village. At the first muted roar
the elder runs in squealing then stops in the kitchen,
her eyes adjusting to the dimness, looking foolish
and unsure. I drop the spoon and bag of peas
and leave her frightened and tittering, wiping my hands
on my jeans, trying to walk and not run,
because I don't want to scare the baby
who's still sat on the patio alone, looking for her sister,
bewildered, trying to figure why she's gone –
all this in the odd, dead pause of the lag –
then sound catches up with the plane
and now its grey belly's right over our house
with a metallic, grinding scream
like the sky's being chainsawed open
and the baby's face drops to a square of pure fear,
she tips forward and flattens her body on the ground
and presses her face into the concrete slab.
I scoop her up and she presses in shuddering,
screaming her strange, *halt* pain cry
and it's all right now I tell her again and again,
but it's never all right now – Christ have mercy –

my daughter in my arms can't steady me –
always some woman is running to catch up her children,
we dig them out of the rubble in parts like plaster dolls –
Mary Mother of God have mercy, mercy on us all.

ACKNOWLEDGEMENTS

Many thanks to the Authors' Foundation for a grant.

Acknowledgements and thanks are due to the editors of the following:

Granta, The Moth, The New Humanist, The New Statesman, Poetry London, The Poetry Review, Wild Court.

'Ace of Bass' is for Andrew McMillan. Huge thanks to Alice Haworth-Booth for her typographical setting of '[transformation: Cyane]'. '[transformation: Callisto]' is for Patricia Millner. 'dear comrade of the boarding house' owes a formal debt to Julia Copus's 'This Is the Poem in which I Have Not Left You' from *The World's Two Smallest Humans* (Faber, 2012). 'Beatitude' was commissioned by Shakespeare's Globe for their 'Voice and Echo' series, and is in part a tribute to Gerard Manley Hopkins. 'Blue Heron' is for David-Antoine Williams and Mira Novek. 'Song for the Rabbit Man' was commissioned for *The Caught Habits of Language: an Entertainment for W. S. Graham for Him Having Reached 100*, eds, Rachael Boast, Andy Ching and Nathan Hamilton (Donut Press, 2018). 'Wildebeest' is for Rose, but is also dedicated to Kaddy Benyon, with thanks for her last-minute help! The 'Marcela Sonnets' were commissioned by *Wild Court*. 'Moon' draws on the story 'The Children Are Sent to Throw the Sleeping Sun into the Sky', from *The Girl Who Made Stars and Other Bushmen Stories*, collected by Wilhelm Bleek and Lucy C. Lloyd, ed., Gregory McNamee (Daimon Folklore Library, 2012) ; I wish to honour and acknowledge the original teller (the stories are unattributed). 'Love Poem, Lucca' and 'Portrait of our Daughters' are both for James Meredith. 'Heavenly Bodies' is for Mark Haworth-Booth.

Thanks to: Jane and David Benson, Aaron Biggins, Tamsin Coe, Jenny Day, Amy Greig, Selina Scott, Tracy Weekes.

Louise Walsh, fellow poet, mum and villager, without whom the juggle of the last four years would have been almost impossible.

Dr Lynne Anderson.

Rachael Allen, Kaddy Benyon, Clare Bullock, Damian and Molly Furniss, Helen Grime, Mark Haworth-Booth, Andrew McMillan, Patricia Millner, Peter Straus, Matthew Turner, David-Antoine Williams.

Julia Copus, many, many times over, and the spectacular Helyars, especially Claire Crowther, Jane Draycott, Annie Freud and Jenny Lewis.

My editor Robin Robertson.

Most of all and always, thanks and love to my husband James Meredith, and our two daughters Isla and Rose. For everything.